Papier Mâché

Papier Mâché

Robin Capon

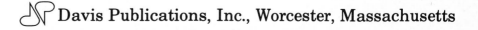 Davis Publications, Inc., Worcester, Massachusetts

1   Papier mâché bedstead with lacquered brass
mounts. Original canopy with valances of cotton
rep trimmed with cords and wood tassels bound
with silk. Probably made in Birmingham about
1850. Gift of HM Queen Mary
Victoria and Albert Museum, Crown Copyright

© Robin Capon 1977
First published 1977
ISBN 0-87192-090-5
Library of Congress Catalog Card Number: 76-39676

Filmset in 10 on 12 pt. Monophoto
Century Schoolbook
by Servis Filmsetting Ltd., Manchester
Printed in Great Britain by
The Pitman Press, Bath
for the publishers BT Batsford Ltd.
4 Fitzhardinge Street, London W1H 0AH

10 9 8 7 6 5 4 3 2 1

Contents

Acknowledgment

My thanks are due to the Trustees of the
Victoria and Albert Museum, London for
providing photographs and giving permission
to reproduce figures 1, 2, 3, 4, 16, 66, 79–82,
110, and 126; the Museum of Childhood,
Edinburgh for figure 83 and for the jacket
photograph; the Royal Scottish Museum,
Edinburgh for figure 111; and Elizabeth Leyh
for figures 121 and 122.

Robin Capon
Maidstone 1977

Foreword

The main consideration of this book is to provide information on papier mâché techniques; the emphasis throughout is on methods and ideas.

Although individual sections of the book may be studied in isolation, it will be necessary to refer back to the first few sections which cover the basic procedures and technical details. To save space and avoid repetition this basic information is not included in subsequent sections. It is therefore particularly important that the reader studies Section 2 before turning to any special technique. The index and list of contents will provide other means of cross-reference and the reader is asked to follow up references mentioned in the text.

2 Chair, wood and japanned papier mâché with mother of pearl inlay, mid nineteenth century *Victoria and Albert Museum, Crown Copyright*

1 Introduction

Papier mâché is of French derivation and probably originates from the French émigré workers of the London papier mâché shops of the eighteenth century. A literal translation of the words is 'chewed paper', a reference to the technique of soaking paper in water to produce a pulp. Similarly, strips or even whole sheets of paper which have been soaked in glue become workable and can be used to create exciting sculptural forms or for application over existing objects. Perhaps with the spiralling cost of manufactured goods and the desire to re-use or re-cycle waste material such as paper, coupled with the increasing interest in crafts and leisure pursuits, papier mâché will experience something of a revival.

Papier mâché has a long history, being among the most ancient of art forms. Objects which are at least 2000 years old have been discovered, proving the durability of the medium. The toughness of the finished product does not preclude individuality in styling and working and for this reason papier mâché has always been used for masks and festival objects and has found an important place in carnivals, pageants, and religious and pagan festivals of all kinds. The Chinese were probably the first to use paper in this way, one early use being for war helmets. Later the Persians and Japanese used it, but it was in Europe during the seventeenth century that wider application of the technique began to be employed. In the extravagant Baroque era papier mâché stage props were used in the theatre and at court. England began to

develop a papier mâché industry, and by the nineteenth century this was using mechanised processes to mass-produce a variety of lacquered and japanned articles, ranging from boxes and trays to large items of furniture. Often the objects were richly ornamented and inlaid with mother-of-pearl. It is reputed that even bungalows were constructed from papier mâché and exported to Australia! Fortunately many fine examples of this period have survived in our museums.

However, papier mâché techniques were not invented for a production line and obviously in modern times mass-production methods have employed more durable and practical materials such as wood, metal and plastic. A further disadvantage of papier mâché furniture is that it tends to be lightweight and therefore possibly unstable; a chair, for example, could easily be knocked over. Yet in America the technique survived as a craft practised by the women settlers who made lamps, boxes, plaques and other useful domestic objects. In Mexico, papier mâché is still used for traditional dolls, masks and colourful festival decorations as well as in production techniques involving specially prepared moulds, which produce a variety of decorative objects for an American market.

The duplication of objects should be left to the liquid plastic on the monotonous mass-production line. Papier mâché is a craft and as such should combine discipline with personality. The materials we use always impose certain limitations; every material has characteristics which must be appreciated and respected. Yet there is always room for the craftsman to express some of his personality in the work, perhaps in the way that he interprets a particular subject or uses colour and form. There is in effect a degree of freedom, the freedom of the individual working with his hands and something which is denied in predetermined methods of production. Creative crafts follow no definite rules, so there is scope for individual research and adaptation.

For handmade objects the advantages of papier mâché are that paper and glue, the basic materials, are familiar to everyone and are inexpensive, adaptable and readily available. Papier mâché is an extremely worthwhile craft which can be both practical and creative. For three-dimensional expression this technique is unrivalled as a cheap yet versatile material. Little is required in the way of tools and materials and the various methods are easy to follow, making the craft suitable for all age groups. Adults might appreciate the freedom the medium offers for sculpture or the precision it can afford for reproducing shapes from a mould. Children are often fascinated by the work and can produce results of surprising originality and quality. As with clay, the direct, physical contact with the material is a property which many find stimulating and satisfying.

The principle of papier mâché is that pasted paper becomes extraordinarily hard when it dries. However, in its wet form it is

very pliable and this means that intricate work is possible which will nevertheless dry to a firm state. There are three basic forms: modelling pulp; pasted strips or sheets of paper used over a mould or applied directly to cover an object; or pasted paper which is crumpled and freely shaped. The aim of this book is to show how each of these methods can be carried out to produce a variety of work. The versatility of the medium means that it can easily be adapted for use in studio, home or classroom, whether for a string of small beads or a large piece of sculpture.

Three-dimensional work is desirable in any art context and the adaptability of papier mâché makes it a most useful material for modelling and appreciating

3   Papier mâché table, kidney-shaped with 'Elizabethan' style legs. English *c.* 1851
Victoria and Albert Museum, Crown Copyright

4   Pair of pole screens, signed on the panel Jennens and Bettridge
Victoria and Albert Museum, Crown Copyright

form. Such work will normally require painting or finishing in some way and so will inevitably link the graphic arts of painting and design with three-dimensional forms. Good design and colour sense is always important. By applying modern paint finishes to a papier mâché surface even greater variety and durability is possible. The modern craftsman has a range of papers, glues, epoxy resins, polyurethanes, acrylics, antiquing materials and spray paints from which to select, making the possibilities for papier mâché work all the more extensive and exciting.

5　A selection of papier mâché articles including a model and a string of beads which were made from pulp

2   Tools, materials and technical notes

As with any craft, the sensible, inexperienced student will start with a simple project which will give him the feel of the basic materials and experience of a single, important technique. Papier mâché is no exception to this and an ideal starting point is to make a small bowl using strips of paper over a plastic or glass original, as described in detail at the beginning of Section 4 of this book. Thus, to start with, a supply of newspaper, some paste, a bucket, a large brush, the mould and some paint are the only essentials. The paste can be of a branded variety such as *Polycell* (wheat paste) or can be made from a flour and water mixture, as detailed on page 18. The main requirements will be readily available in most homes and the cost of beginning work in papier mâché will therefore be minimal.

Papier mâché work need not involve a mess but nevertheless it is useful to have a working surface which can be devoted entirely to the work whilst in its various stages of production. This is a craft which needs time, patience and disciplined methods of working. A table with a washable surface is ideal. An old table covered with oilcloth or sheets of newspaper is equally good, otherwise use the kitchen or dining room table but ensure that it is adequately protected before starting work. If work in progress cannot be left on the table then obviously additional storage space must be found elsewhere. Incidentally, old cupboards, bookcases, orange crates and wooden boxes can provide useful storage space. Always check that materials are available in sufficient quantity and that all necessary tools are to hand before beginning work.

As the student gains confidence and experience so he will wish to tackle more complex and adventurous projects which will no doubt involve additional equipment to that listed above. The detailed technical information which follows is fundamental to subsequent sections of this book and serves as an essential guide and background to procedures which are later dealt with in detail.

Basic equipment
Containers of different sizes are among the first essential items of equipment. Plastic buckets are desirable in which to mix the paste, whilst smaller jars and screw-top containers can be used for the mixing and storage of paint. Lids from jars and tins can likewise act as palettes. Jars, bottles, buckets and plastic containers of various types are always useful as basic moulds over which to work.

A pair of sharp scissors and a craft knife should always be available, as should pencils, a ruler and brushes of different types and sizes. A bradawl, pliers, palette knife, sponges, masking tape and transparent adhesive tape (*sellotape* or *scotch tape*) could also be required. Papier mâché puppets and masks can involve wire, wire mesh, hardboard (*masonite*), balsa wood, balloons, plastic bottles, polystyrene (*styrofoam*) and cardboard or cardboard tubes (mailing tubes) as supports or armatures. Other items, such

6 Useful containers

as fabric, string, yarn, veneer, small shells, printed papers and 'found objects' could be used in decorating basic papier mâché forms. The use of a potter's wheel, banding wheel or turntable is an advantage when applying decoration or finishes to a bowl or similar symmetrical papier mâché object.

Different techniques will require different materials and equipment. Those not mentioned in this general list will be specified in the appropriate part of the book. Papers, glues and sealing agents are essential in all the work and information on these important materials is detailed under following headings.

7 Some basic equipment

Papers

It is sometimes surprising how much paper is required for a single project. Newspaper is the most useful and the papier mâché enthusiast will always have a large stock of old newspapers in hand. Newspaper can vary considerably in quality, not only in thickness and strength but also in the surface characteristics of the paper and in the amount and type of ink used. Obviously one is tempted to use those most readily available but avoid newspapers which have a great deal of bold type and heavy inking. If the ink offsets when the paper is wetted this will not only affect the gluing stage of the work but can make the surface difficult to prime and decorate. Many magazines use a similar type of paper but avoid the smooth paper of the more expensive 'glossy' magazines. In addition newspaper is, of course, most useful for covering tables and protecting surfaces whilst work is in progress. White newsprint, white brushwork paper, kitchen paper and ceiling or lining paper are similar types and can be used for the final layer over ordinary newspaper so as to establish a white or clear surface on which to work.

Heavier papers are useful for papier mâché sculpture and modelling. Cartridge (drawing) paper is ideal, although it is becoming rather expensive. Various other papers make good pulp: these include newspapers, sugar paper (bogus paper), corrugated papers and other soft types used for packing or as containers for eggs and fruit.

8   Various papers and paper pulp

Paper towelling, crêpe paper and tissue papers respond well to creasing (froissage), bunching and overlapping techniques and can be used to create a textured finish to the surface of an object. Colour contrasts can be exploited by using strips or squares of different coloured tissue which are made to overlap.

Gummed papers, construction paper, detail paper, brown wrapping paper, gift wrapping paper, wallpaper, hand-printed papers and paper bags are among other kinds which can be employed effectively.

Some kinds of paper respond better to a certain use or technique than do others, therefore always check that you have sufficient quantity of the correct paper at hand before beginning work. Heavier papers

9 Tearing strips of newspaper against a straight-edge

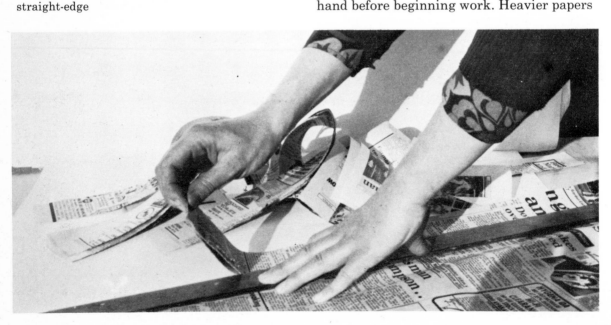

work better if they are soaked in water for a few minutes before placing them in the glue medium. Except when precise shapes are required for collage decoration or masking, always *tear* the paper to the approximate shape desired. The torn edge adheres better, is easier to sandpaper and will help produce a stronger finished article. Papers tear most easily with the grain; tearing across the grain will prove more difficult and will result in a ragged and uneven edge. Strips of paper can be torn against a straight-edge. Most work involving layers of glued paper applied over an armature or mould will require strips about 25 mm (1 in.) wide. An alternative is to build up the form by using squares about 38 mm (1½ in.). The number of layers may vary with different techniques and according to what is being made. Detailed explanations of these different methods and requirements are given in later sections of this book.

10 Tearing small squares of newspaper from strips

Instant mâché
Instant papier mâché is a commercial product which is retailed through many art and craft stores. It is normally available in dry form in a strong polythene container. When required, water is added and the mixture is kneaded until it has a workable 'feel' or consistency like that of firm clay. Instant mâché tends to dry rather slowly and does not stick to plastic, a quality which can be exploited if a plastic object is used as a mould. Instant mâché is an excellent sculptural medium; in its wet state it behaves in a similar way to modelling clay

and when dry it can be cut to shape with a knife or saw, drilled and sandpapered.

11   Various adhesives

Glues

Forms can be made simply from moistened newspaper or pulp and indeed this can work quite satisfactorily, but the addition of glue or paste will give greater strength and durability to the papier mâché object. Today there is a large variety of glues available from suppliers, craft shops and hardware or Do-it-yourself stores and most of these are suitable. Some glues adhere harder than others, so consider the function of the object being made and the type of paper being used. A papier mâché object such as a waste-paper basket which will have daily use, will need to use a strong bonding agent such as an epoxy resin or polymer medium, whilst a model or something decorative could use a cheaper paste.

FLOUR AND WATER PASTE

This is suitable for almost all but the heaviest papers, and will suit most methods. It can be made to either of the following two recipes:

1 *Pour 1 cup of water into a plastic bowl or glass jar and slowly add ¼ cup of flour to make a thin mixture. Stir this mixture into 5 cups of lightly boiling water. Continue boiling and stirring for a further 3 minutes. Cool for use.*
2 *Mix ½ cup flour with ¼ cup powdered casein glue (or less of wallpaper paste or wheat paste) and add this little by little to 1 pint of warm water, stirring continuously. Stir until the paste has a smooth, even consistency.*

The second recipe will produce a thicker, stronger paste than the first. This paste will not keep for very long so try not to make more than is necessary for a particular session or item of work.

WALLPAPER PASTE (WHEAT PASTE)

Polycell and various other brand names are available from hardware stores and decorators' merchants. Mix according to the instructions on the packet; a small packet will usually make one gallon of paste. Add the powder gradually to the necessary amount of *warm* water, stirring until it has completely dissolved. Wallpaper paste will keep for some time, especially if stored in an airtight container, but again, it is pointless to mix more than is really necessary. Most varieties incorporate a fungicide which prevents the formation of mould whilst the article is drying out. Wallpaper paste can also be used to size or seal a papier mâché surface prior to painting or decorating.

PVA MEDIUM (POLYVINYL ACETATE ADHESIVE)

Polymer mediums, sometimes known as white paste, are now manufactured by all of the large art suppliers. Pva medium is probably the most versatile of all glues available. It will stick most materials, is quick-drying, can be used as a sealant and varnish and has the advantage that brushes and containers are easily cleaned by rinsing them in water. For papier mâché work the polymer medium can be diluted by adding not more than one part water to three parts glue; for really strong and durable results, use the glue in its neat state. The most economical quantity to buy is a gallon container (4546 cc), and most manufacturers will be willing to supply this by post if it is not locally available. A comprehensive list of suppliers is given on page 92. In America, white emulsion glue, such as *Elmer's, Wilhold* and *Sobo*, has similar properties and can be used in the same way.

OTHER GLUES

Epoxy is recommended by some enthusiasts as the best glue and certainly it will produce a finish which is remarkably rigid, virtually unbreakable and water, flame, burn and stain proof. It is most useful for gluing on decorative items to the basic papier mâché article; it dries slowly but transparently. Epoxy is expensive and therefore not recommended for large scale projects. Epoxy resin glues are available under many brand names, such as *Dunlop Epoxy Adhesive, Bostik No.* 7 and *Araldite*. Unwanted resin is much more difficult to remove from a surface than its water-based equivalent (pva), and must be diluted with paint thinners, or failing that, nail-varnish remover.

In the absence of a polymer adhesive, other household glues, such as *Copydex, Bostik, Evo-stik* and *Uhu*, can be useful for materials which require a stronger adhesive.

Vegetable glue is best for gluing fabrics which might be used as decorative trim or for lining the inside of a papier mâché box or the base of an ornament.

Marketed paper glues such as *Gloy* have similar characteristics to wallpaper paste but used in quantity these tend to be expensive.

Gluing

Use strong plastic buckets in which to mix

12   Dip application of glue

the glue. If a powdered type is being used, then ensure that it completely dissolves; agitate the mixture frequently with a stick or whisk so as to prevent the formation of lumps. A simple whisk can be made by bending and intertwining two wire coat-hangers. Other glues may need diluting. For most projects a quantity of glue will be required so for convenience mix or pour out the necessary amount into a plastic container. One can always make more; it is better to underestimate the amount needed rather than have a surplus. Select the glue to suit the types of paper being used and the method of working. A glue mixture is also required for making pulp, and this is described in detail on page 59.

There are two methods of gluing:
Dip application is most suitable when strips of paper are being used. Each strip is pulled through a quantity of glue in a tray or bucket so as to completely saturate it. As the strip, dripping with glue, is removed, so it is placed on the surface to be covered and brushed over to ensure good adhesion.
Brush application suits a variety of methods. A large, soft, flat brush such as a 50 mm (2 in.) decorators' brush should be used to apply glue to strips or squares being used to build up objects. Large sheets of paper used for modelling or sculpture can be pasted similarly. Always ensure that the paper is generously coated with glue. Do the gluing on a formica or similar washable surface or on sheets of newspaper which can simply be thrown away afterwards. When a sufficient number of layers has been applied

20

to form the papier mâché surface, brush a final coating of glue over the whole area. This will help seal the surface and will ensure that all edges are firmly pasted down.

After use, thoroughly rinse and clean all brushes and containers. Do not allow the brushes to become hard before attempting to clean them, nor is it a good idea to leave them to stand in water or turpentine for any length of time as this will eventually distort the bristles. Brushes used for pastes, pva adhesives and vegetable glue can be rinsed clean in warm water. Those used for epoxy and other household glues will need to be cleaned in turpentine or paint thinners. Brushes are expensive and it is as well to take good care of them.

Drying

The importance of allowing the work to dry out between various stages of a project is often underestimated. Glued papers must be thoroughly dry before sealing or painting is attempted. Papier mâché is a time-consuming craft and undue haste will normally result only in disappointment.

The length of time a particular piece of work will take to dry will depend on various factors. The kinds of paper and glue used will influence the drying time, as will the number of layers applied and the temperature and conditions in which the object is allowed to dry. Some papers are more absorbent than others; one layer of paper could dry in a matter of hours whilst several layers could take days.

The drying process can be hastened in a

13   Brush application of glue

14 Supporting an object left to dry

number of ways. For instance, placing the object in the sun or by a hot radiator or air-vent will speed the drying. In such cases ensure that air can freely circulate around the article and rotate it periodically so that one part does not dry out much faster than another. Wet papier mâché objects can also be force-dried in an oven by making use of the heat remaining after cooking, by simply using the heat from the pilot light in a gas oven, or by operating the oven at a low temperature. Obviously there is a risk with these methods of damaging the objects or even causing a fire, so progress should be checked frequently. Very fast drying can cause the object to warp.

Items made with wallpaper paste (wheat paste) tend to dry slower than others and in this case it may be advantageous to use artificial methods.

When leaving it to dry, place the object on a clean surface and one to which it will not stick. If necessary, use wax paper or support the object on props or wire mesh.

Waterproofing
With certain objects it will be an advantage to make them impervious to water, and when this is so the simplest method is to coat or soak the papier mâché in raw linseed oil. This will also increase the strength and durability of the articles.
Method: having completed the first stage of the work, the entire surface of the dry papier mâché article is coated with linseed oil. Apply this first coat lightly, working the oil into the surface. Allow the article to stand

for about an hour. Much of the first coating of linseed oil will have seeped into the paper. Now apply a generous second coating but check that the oil does not run and thus form ridges. Place the article in an oven and bake at not more than 250°C until it is completely dry.

Using an epoxy resin adhesive will also render the object waterproof, as will a lacquer, gloss or varnish finish.

Sealing

Normally the papier mâché surface will need to be painted or decorated in some way and must therefore be prepared by priming or sealing. This practice will give a hard finish to the paper, will prevent print from bleeding through and will make the surface less absorbent to future coats of paint.

Size, wallpaper paste and branded primers can be used. Size and paste can be mixed with powder colour, temperacolour or other water-based paints, so that the primed surface can also form a background colour for decoration. Emulsion, acrylic, latex and craft paints are thicker, have excellent covering qualities and will act as a primer, allowing the work to dry between each application and smoothing with very fine sandpaper before repainting. Textured finishes can be achieved by adding fine sand or sawdust to the primer and if desired striating the surface with a comb.

Undiluted polymer adhesive also acts as a good sealer but, of course, this dries transparent and therefore the newsprint will show through. If a plain surface is desired then add a final layer of white newsprint, lining (ceiling) paper, or sketch paper before sealing with polymer adhesive, pva or white glue. Alternatively, mix some colour into the adhesive, or paint over the dried, glued surface with a polymer, acrylic, latex or craft paint.

Experiments can be made with various other media, such as a weak plaster/size/paint/water mixture, or *Polyfilla* (*Spackle*)/paint/water mixture. These mixtures should be brushed on thinly, applying a succession of coats, drying and sandpapering between each. Remember that moisture is the real enemy of papier mâché, so do not apply paints and primers too liberally. Check that the sealing technique being used will suit later applications of paint or other methods of decorating and finishing. Water-based decoration, for example, will not be compatible with an underlying oil-based primer.

Handling the object whilst it is being primed can become a problem. With a symmetrical object it is an advantage to have the use of a turntable so that the object can be rotated as it is painted. Alternatively, the article can be supported on an empty upturned can or even a bottle, so that the underside edges can be reached easily. Allow the primer to dry before overpainting. Primers dry best at room temperature; force drying can cause cracking. Clean brushes immediately after use.

Using gesso

Gesso can be made in a number of ways but

is basically a mixture of animal glue or size and whiting. It is a white, opaque substance which dries rock-hard. Gesso can be sandpapered and smoothed to a very fine finish and will provide a pleasant surface on which to paint. Like size and pva adhesive, it will help strengthen the papier mâché object.

Gesso may be obtained in a can, as powder in a box, or it can be made by mixing 1 part whiting with 1 part 1:7 glue size mixture (1 part size to 7 parts water).

Liquid gesso poured from a can is possibly the easiest to use. Pour some of the liquid into a plastic bowl and then brush it over the papier mâché surface. Use several coats, allowing each one to dry before applying the next. Gesso is best used over heavier, textured paper surfaces; it may crack if allowed to dry too fast or if applied to a very smooth surface. Overpainting with one or two further layers of gesso will usually successfully cover up any cracking. Brushes should be rinsed in warm water immediately after use. Add some water to the can of gesso so as to keep it workable; do not mix the water with the gesso but simply let it lie on the top so that it is easily poured off before re-use.

Powdered gesso is mixed with water to obtain a smooth, creamy consistency before being brushed on. Follow the same procedure mentioned above.

To make gesso from a whiting/glue size mixture begin by sieving the dry whiting powder into a little of the hot size until a thick, smooth paste is formed. Add the rest of the size, keeping the mixture warm in a double boiler.

Gesso can be coloured by mixing it with powder or tempera paint.

Barbola Paste is manufactured by Winsor and Newton and has similar properties to gesso. See Suppliers List, page 92.

Painting

Papier mâché articles can be brush, spray, dip or offset painted and today there is a great variety of paints available. As with other stages, it is necessary to work carefully; whatever method is used the paint should be applied thinly, using as many layers as necessary and leaving the work to dry between each application. Check the suitability of paint to primer and whether combinations of paint are compatible and will allow intermixing and overpainting.

Methods will necessitate constraint and careful thought must be given to the selection of colours, designs and motifs, yet this is the stage of the work which allows the greatest freedom for individual expression and inventiveness. The painting and decoration of the papier mâché will have the most significant effect on the impact of the completed object.

Brush application is suitable for most paints, selecting the size and type of brush in relation to the size of the object, its surface characteristics, and whether a broad or detailed treatment is desired. For flat areas of background colour use a large, soft-haired, decorators' brush, and for details use a pointed sable hair brush. Many types of enamels, lacquers, acrylics and cellulose paints can now be obtained in aerosol cans and will give interesting matt and gloss effects using different spray techniques. For example, specific shapes can be masked out prior to spraying by using thin paper templates wetted on to the papier mâché surface; a design can be built up by combining this method with superimposed layers of different colours. The paper template must be no more than slightly wetted and should be peeled off as soon as the surrounding paint has dried. Diluted paint can be used with a spray-gun, air brush, or spray diffuser. Always spray in a well-ventilated room, if possible placing the article in an old cardboard box to prevent the surplus spray drifting too far. Again, it is an advantage to have the article on a turntable. Other methods include partial dipping or total immersion of the object in liquid paint or dye, as used with wax-resist designing, and offsetting paint on to the papier mâché by means of stick blocks, potato blocks, lengths of card, sponges and so on.

Powder (tempera) paint is inexpensive and is probably the most suitable for use by children. This paint is mixed with water to the desired consistency, the colours readily intermix and easily take to the papier mâché surface. Powder paint can be flicked, stippled or brushed on, but tends to crack if used too thickly. Poster paints and designers' gouache are useful for smaller objects or detailed work, but on the whole traditional water-based paints are not

15   Various paints

suitable for papier mâché; they do not cover well and they mark and stain easily unless protected by several coats of varnish.

Similarly, artists' oil paint is equally unsuitable as it is difficult to use and dries slowly. Other opaque finishes can be achieved with lacquer, which is the traditional finish for papier mâché, acrylic, latex, emulsion and enamel paints. Acrylic and latex paints are easy to use, dilute in water, and are fast-drying, but some of the colours do not respond to intermixing and can be rather crude. Use clear lacquer for a transparent paint finish.

For unusual finishes, antique sprays, silver paint and fluorescent paints can be used. Antiquing will give a metallic look to the object and works best on a textured surface. Metallic spray paints such as copper and gold are used as a base and the result can be enhanced by using gold metal leaf and overworking with brown shellac varnish.

Decorating

Although the painted surface offers many possibilities, it need only be the background for a variety of other decorative and finishing techniques. Indeed, the completed item need not be painted at all. The obvious alternative to painting is to employ a collage technique and it will therefore be necessary

16 Fire screen: papier mâché, black and gold on dark red ground. Centre panel painted with scene of a country mansion. Made by Jennens and Bettridge, mid nineteenth century
Victoria and Albert Museum, Crown Copyright

to have a suitable adhesive available to attach the various materials to the paper surface. Quick-drying impact adhesives are generally the most useful. If working over a painted background, avoid marking the paint by over-gluing or spilling.

Strips of lace or fabric and lengths of string or cord are most useful and will enhance a flat painted surface by providing contrasts of line, colour and texture. Other collage effects can be achieved by using overlapped tissue paper shapes, paper doilies, or by a montage or découpage technique using contrasts of colours and textures. Painted papers and wallpapers are also useful and simple printmaking techniques can be used to provide designs especially for this purpose. Potato-printed papers can be most effective. Relief effects can be explored with corrugated papers and textured and embossed wallpapers, or by mounting folded cardboard shapes, lengths of balsa wood and similar materials on to the papier mâché surface. Shells and other decorative items can be set into a plaster surface, which also offers possibilities for engraved designs whilst it is still moist.

Ball-point and felt-tip (fibre-tip) pens and drawing inks are among other media which can be used effectively.

Varnishing

Matt and gloss varnishes may be used as a final protective coating over both painted and collaged finishes. Gloss varnish will enrich the underlying colours and all varnishes will help protect surfaces from

17 A selection of varnishes

marks and stains. Select the varnish to suit the particular painted or paper surface. As with priming and painting, always apply smooth, thin coats, allowing each to dry before revarnishing; thick coatings of varnish will crack. Several coats will be required to give a really glossy finish. Wet varnish attracts dust, so try to find the cleanest and most dust-free conditions in which to work; it is sometimes a better policy to varnish out-of-doors. Most varnishes tend to lie on the surface and, as they dry by oxidation rather than evaporation, they have a lengthy drying time. If the papier mâché object is for outdoor use or has to be exposed to wet or damp conditions then it should certainly be varnished.

Paper surfaces can be varnished with any type of paper varnish, diluted polymer adhesive (matt), poster varnish spray, or clear household varnish, although this may 'yellow' slightly.

Papier mâché objects which are going to be subjected to much wear and tear or which are for outdoor use or decoration should be protected with paints containing acrylic resins, epoxies or a polyurethane varnish. Epoxy finishes are now available in clear and coloured varieties. Some are premixed for spray or brush application, others have two containers, one containing the colour and one the catalyst. These two components are not mixed until one is ready to use the liquid epoxy finish. This is another product which must be used with great care and according to the manufacturer's instructions.

Wear rubber gloves, avoid contact with the skin, and work in a well-ventilated room. If epoxy is spilled on the skin, wash the affected area immediately with alcohol and rinse thoroughly with soap and water.

High gloss enamel and liquid porcelain can also be used as protective finishes. Shellac varnish is useful for a quick-drying finish as, like lacquer, it dries partly into the surface of the papier mâché. Shellac is available as a clear white varnish or in an orange/brown form; it is thinned with denatured alcohol. Shellac should not be used as a finish for objects which are to be exposed to water or alcohol.

Most varnishes can be diluted by using the appropriate solvent or thinning agent: acrylic solvent, paint thinners, turpentine, or water. These are also used for cleaning brushes and equipment. Incidentally, it is wise to use good quality brushes for applying the varnish; cheap brushes tend to shed hairs and thus spoil the finish. Always replace the lid tightly on a tin of varnish and store it upside-down to prevent the formation of a skin.

Basic procedures

Good results are usually the product of an organised and disciplined approach. The preceding information has been set out in the order in which one would normally work: checking of equipment, use of paper and glue, allowing the work to dry, priming, painting and decorating, and varnishing. This information will apply to all the basic papier mâché techniques, whether working over existing objects, producing items from moulds, using paper pulp, pasting large sheets of paper for modelling, or making papier mâché sculpture, masks and puppets. These techniques are now covered in detail, but for technical information the reader should always refer to this section of the book and consult the index and suppliers list. Each of the subsequent sections of this book is illustrated with photographs showing basic procedures as well as examples of finished papier mâché articles. The reader may wish to base his own work on these, adapt them, or use them as inspiration for other work. Obviously each example is open to numerous possibilities, especially in the way that it is painted and decorated.

3   Using existing objects

An excellent starting point for papier mâché work is to cover an existing object. With this method the selected object forms a ready-made foundation for papier mâché, which is added to strengthen and modify it. The original object remains permanently under the papier mâché. The advantages for the beginner are that he works to a given form or shape and therefore does not have to work out a design, and that he does not confront the problems of removing the papier mâché from the original. He can therefore work quickly and directly, experiencing some of the fundamental procedures and the 'feel' of the basic materials. This is a method for producing individual items rather than one for duplicating forms; where several identical shapes are required it is necessary to work from a mould, as described in the next section of this book.

It may seem an extravagance to permanently cover something with papier mâché, perhaps even a pointless exercise. Obviously useful household objects are not employed, but rather those which we normally discard. It is surprising what a variety of shapes become available if all the different cardboard packages, cartons, boxes, plastic bottles and canisters, tins and polystyrene containers are saved from the waste bin for possible use in papier mâché work. Such items can be strengthened with layers of papier mâché and subsequently painted and decorated to make more durable and useful articles or attractive, decorative objects. The basic shape can be modified by a build up of mâché in particular areas, by modelling over part of the surface with paper pulp, or by gluing a number of basic shapes together. The number of layers or thickness of pulp which can be applied to a given basic form without it unduly warping will be determined by the thickness and strength of the original material. Working over a metal surface, for example, will allow greater scope than that of a thin cardboard container. Also, of course, it is possible to alter the shape of the original carton or article by cutting part of it away. For example, a plastic bottle can be turned into a cylindrical container simply by removing the top with a sharp pair of scissors or a craft knife. Other objects can be given a new lease of life by resurfacing with papier mâché and decorating and varnishing appropriately.

Method of working

Ensure that the surface of the selected item is clean, dry and will suitably take the adhesive to be used. Use a stronger adhesive such as pva (white glue) on metal and polystyrene (styrofoam) surfaces. Check that the edges of metal and plastic items are smooth; if necessary, file or sandpaper them.

Cover the surface of the original item with strips or squares of pasted paper. Build up with several layers of paper, applying each in a different direction, see figures 19 to 21. The number of layers will depend on the strength of the basic item and the function of the completed object. Two layers will be sufficient over thin cardboard boxes whilst more can be applied to plastic and tin containers. Obviously the resultant weight of a number of layers coupled with the consequent amount of moisture and glue could produce warping. Some enthusiasts would suggest that warping is an inherent, almost necessary, quality which adds to the charm and character of papier mâché, whilst others would argue that if an article is designed and made for a specific purpose it may need to be symmetrical or follow some particular line or shape. Certainly, if precautions are taken, warping can normally be avoided. Warping is often the result of uneven drying, force drying, an excess of glue, incompatibility between papier mâché and basic shape or mould, or possible other factors when working over a mould, see page 44. Where, as in this case, the papier mâché is applied directly over an object, ensure that the first layer is generously pasted and is going to stick to the base surface. If in doubt, use a pva adhesive, as this will stick paper to any surface. If the papier mâché is built up over a thin cardboard article it may be necessary to pad out the inside of the article with dry paper, or weight it in some way to prevent warping whilst the object dries. Check the surface for lumps and air pockets; squeeze out excess glue and press flat. Allow the object to dry out thoroughly. If required, the surface may then be smoothed by using a very fine grade sandpaper. The object can be primed, painted and decorated in the usual way, as detailed in Section 2 of this book.

Figures 22 to 44 illustrate work produced

18 A selection of 'waste' containers which are suitable for overworking with papier mâché

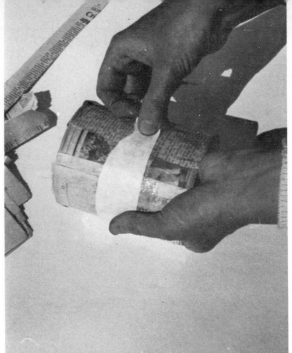

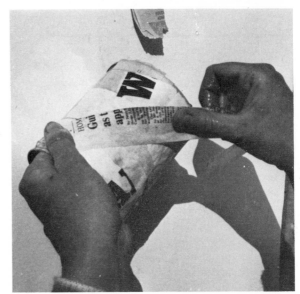

19–21   Method of overworking an empty tin with
papier mâché strips
Each layer of strips is applied in a different
direction

by covering existing objects with papier mâché. The majority of these articles were made from common household waste, tins, bottles and the like, using this simple technique to transform the original into something useful and attractive. Similar methods include covering an armature to make papier mâché sculpture, and working over a balloon to make a mask. These ideas are explained in detail in later sections of this book.

The canister illustrated in figures 23 to 25 was worked in papier mâché over a flimsy plastic original. Many foods, particularly freezer foods, are sold in such containers and these are easily strengthened with pasted strips and can be decorated and varnished to provide a useful and attractive article. When working over plastic, pva adhesive (white glue) is recommended for the first layer, as this will adhere better to the original. It will only be necessary to apply two or three layers of paper.

Overworked glass jars (ketchup, salad cream, pickles, etc) make useful vases, see figures 27 to 30. Again, only a couple of layers of paper is necessary. If painted in water paints, the design must be varnished to prevent it being marked by handling and drips of water.

Empty cardboard containers such as those illustrated in figures 31 and 32 can be decorated by découpage, using wallpaper, printed papers, stamps and similar decorative papers. See also Section 10.

Aluminium foil containers make sturdy bases over which to work with papier mâché. Once more, a used container can be turned into something attractive and functional, see figures 39 and 40. Aluminium foil can also be used as a basis for masks and sculpture. See Sections 7 and 8.

22 Some completed articles ready for painting

23 Canister with lid, strengthened with overworked papier mâché and ready for finishing

24 *and* 25 Two variations for decorating the canister illustrated in figure 23

26 Small container with lid. Plastic, covered with papier mâché and decorated with fabric trim.

27 Glass screw-top jar covered with papier mâché and decorated with string motifs

28 As figure 27 painted and varnished

29 Glass jar decorated with fish motif and spray varnished with poster varnish

30 Montage to illustrate the complete design

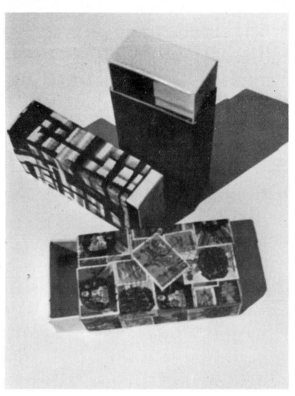

31 Large match boxes covered with various decorative papers

32 Match box container decorated with used postage stamps

33 Empty tin and a container which has been made by covering such a tin with papier mâché. The lid is made from cardboard and cardboard tubing

34 The container illustrated in figure 33 with the lid removed to show the unpainted papier mâché inside and the lid which was made from two circles of cardboard, the inner circle being slightly less in diameter than that of the tin

35 Overworked plastic container. The linear design was impressed, using a length of card dipped in paint. The letters were cut from a magazine and glued to a white surround

36 Container for pencils made from an empty household cleanser container cut to size and covered with two layers of strip papier mâché

37 Cardboard container overworked with tissue paper to obtain a heavy textured effect

38   Other containers worked with tissue paper

39 *and* 40   Used aluminium foil cartons covered with papier mâché and painted

41 Bracelet made by working over a ring of cardboard

42 Cardboard fruit container strengthened with papier mâché

43 Finished version of figure 42 in use as a garden trug

44 Old chair worked over with papier mâché strips. The original seat has been replaced with strong hessian edged with fabric trim. Papier mâché can be applied as découpage; that is the print can form an interesting design in its own right. This can be protected with a suitable paper varnish

4 Using moulds

With this technique a selected article is used as the basis for a papier mâché 'casting'. The papier mâché is applied over the original article or mould but this is removed once the paper has dried. The cast mâché is therefore identical in shape and character to the original mould, which may be used many times. This is not a difficult technique to master and it has the advantage of allowing the creation of an object without permanently covering an original, and also offers the possibility of duplicating articles. Identical forms produced in this way can be decorated and finished differently and so still evolve as individual objects. The dry basic form produced from the mould can be adapted and modified by overworking with paper strips or pulp, or by the addition of handles or similar decorative features.

Many common household articles such as bowls, pots, dishes, plates, trays and flower pots will make suitable moulds. Plastic bowls are excellent since their flexibility is a great advantage when it comes to removing the papier mâché. To facilitate the easy separation of papier mâché, the mould must be simple in shape, widest at the top and gradually sloping in to the base. A smooth surface will be easier to work over than one which is elaborately ridged or embossed. The inside or outer surface of the mould may be used. Other more complex surfaces, for instance plastic toys, can be used as moulds, but in such examples the papier mâché casing has to be cut in half before it can be removed from the mould. The two halves must then be joined with adhesive and further layers of papier mâché to form the completed shape. Moulds can also be made from clay and plaster, ideas which are described on page 49.

Method
The mould should be clean and dry and must be prepared by applying a separating medium so that the papier mâché will not stick to it. A thin coating of petroleum jelly (*Vaseline*) will be suitable for most surfaces, otherwise apply a light dusting of talc or cover with aluminium foil, waxed paper, nonstick sandwich wrap or strips of wet, but not pasted, newspaper. Aluminium foil and sandwich wrap will stick to the papier mâché covering but not to the object. An alternative is simply to carefully lightly paste the first layer of strips and apply these to overlap on each other, with the pasted side uppermost. With methods which use a foil or other type of paper to begin with, the inner surface of the completed papier mâché form will need further attention after removal from the mould. Petroleum jelly is the most reliable separating medium; remember to use this around the rim and along the top part of the inside of the mould so that strips which overlap the rim will also come away easily when a sufficient number of layers has been applied.

Ensure that an adequate supply of paste and paper is available. Tear strips approximately 38 mm (1½ in.) in width and soak these in water prior to pasting. Always use a paste solution such as flour and water paste for the first layer, or alternatively

45 Suitable bowl shape for use as a 'one-piece' mould

46 Curved vase shape which could not be reproduced in one piece. See figures 73 to 77

cover with strips of wet, but not pasted, newspaper. This is a double insurance against the first layer sticking to the mould. Additional layers can use a firmer adhesive, such as pva or white paste. To help form a stronger object each layer should be applied in a different direction. Layers can make use of different types or colours of paper so as to be distinguishable from the one beneath. At least five layers will be required; for real strength and durability up to seven or eight. Remember to work some strips over the edge of the mould, but not to such an extent as to create difficulty in removing the paper mâché from the original. The final layer can be one of white newsprint, a similar thin white paper, or a coloured paper, depending on the type of finish desired.

The strip method is possibly the best for most work using a mould but this does not preclude the use of smaller squares of paper, or pulp. Layers made with squares of approximately 50 mm (2 in.) can be combined with those built up with strips. For a textured finish, a thin coating of paper pulp may be used over preceding layers made with strips of paper.

Figures 47 to 54 illustrate stages in working with pasted strips over a mould.

If the surface of the mould has been adequately prepared then it is far better to allow the papier mâché to dry out before attempting to separate it from the mould. Undue haste in removing work from the mould will probably result in damage. Certainly, an object which is allowed to dry on the mould is less liable to warp than one which is removed whilst it is still wet. However, individual conditions and circumstances must be considered.

Use a flat-bladed knife, a palette knife or spatula to remove the object from the mould. Work round the mould, carefully easing the paper slightly away from the surface. If the original surface was well greased it should be possible to twist or rotate the mould first in one direction and then in the opposite one, so as to slowly work it away from its papier mâché covering. Sometimes a vacuum builds up between the two surfaces and this can be released by piercing through the layers of paper with a strong pin.

The rim of the object will need trimming with sharp scissors and must then be finished and strengthened by pasting small strips across the consequent frayed edge to bind it together, as illustrated in figure 54. Also, now is the time to patch up any faulty or damaged parts of the surface with small pasted squares of paper, and to add handles or make any desired modifications to the basic form. Handles may be attached with an appropriate strong adhesive and further secured with strips of pasted paper. Laminated strips, made by pasting a long strip of paper and then folding this over itself several times to form a shorter, thicker strip, can be used to build up decorative ridges and designs. Ensure that such additions to the basic form are generously pasted and firmly attached. Allow the object to dry out thoroughly before proceeding with sealing and subsequent stages.

47   Applying petroleum jelly to the mould shape

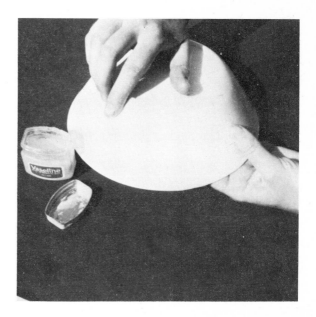

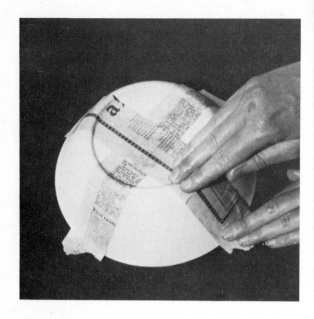

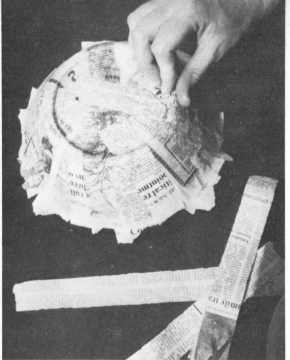

48 Beginning to cover the mould with radiating strips

49 Completed first layer of strips

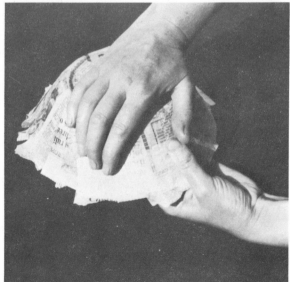

50 Applying strips in a horizontal direction

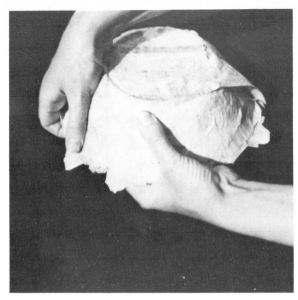

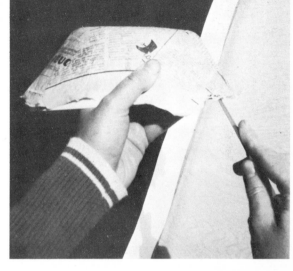

51 The third layer of strips being applied in a diagonal direction

52 Easing the dried papier mâché from the mould with a blunt knife

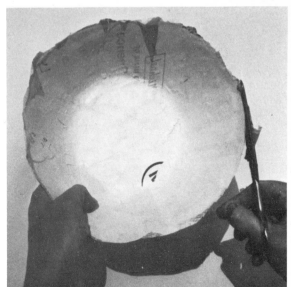

53 Trimming the edges

54 Binding the edges of the papier mâché dish with small strips of pasted paper

55 The completed dish with some useful equipment

Making a plaster mould

Working over plastic bowls, trays, vases and other objects will enable a rich variety of papier mâché shapes to be made but, of course, the form of the finished article is very much determined by the original mould. For the duplication of particular forms and for work of greater individuality, it will be necessary to create a plaster mould. This is, in fact, the most efficient way of reproducing papier mâché pieces and is the method used industrially.

Making a plaster mould is a fairly complex procedure and is therefore really not worth undertaking unless a quantity of articles is desired. As with all objects produced from a mould, each can be decorated and finished in a different way and thus achieve a certain element of individuality. A one-piece mould will produce half a shape, that is to say that the back of the finished casting will be flat if the mould has been filled with paper pulp or open if it has been covered with several layers of papier mâché strips. Such pieces will resemble plaques rather than a fully three-dimensional object which can be viewed from all angles. For complete three-dimensional work it will be necessary to make two moulds so that each forms half of the design of the complete shape. They will have to be so designed that the two shapes fit exactly together, 'back to back' as it were. Two halves made in this way are taped together before sealing and finishing.

METHOD

The form must first be created in clay. Pottery and modelling clays can be used; remember to store these in airtight polythene bags when not in use to prevent them hardening. An alternative is to use plasticine or a similar oil based clay which does not harden readily and can be used over and over again. Work on a clean, flat surface such as a sheet of glass or *formica*. Model the form to produce bold, simple shapes, *without any undercuts* so as to enable the papier mâché to separate easily from the mould. Remember that the cast is always the reverse of the mould. Work over the clay form with flat knife, modelling tools and a wet sponge so as to achieve the desired smooth shape.

Next, the shape must be enclosed in order to contain the plaster which is to cover it. Build a cardboard 'wall' around the clay form using strips of thick cardboard held in place with pieces of clay. Ensure that the height of the cardboard will allow an adequate covering of plaster over the clay. Grease the inside surface of the cardboard with petroleum jelly.

Use plaster of paris, available from chemists and hardware stores, or casting plaster, which may be obtained from craft and ceramic suppliers. Mix the plaster according to the recommendations on the packet. Add the powder to water, mixing to form a thick, creamy consistency. Mix in a plastic bowl, stirring gently with a spatula or spoon. Ensure that no lumps are left in the mixture. Tap the bowl occasionally to make all the air bubbles come to the surface. Pour the plaster carefully over the clay so as to completely cover it to a thickness of at least 13 mm ($\frac{1}{2}$ in.). Allow the plaster to set in room temperature and in draught-free conditions.

When completely dry, remove the cardboard strips reverse the plaster mould and carefully scrape out the clay. Clean the inside with a damp sponge. The mould is now ready for use with papier mâché. The mould should be greased and can then be covered with strips or pulp, following the procedure already outlined for the use of other types of mould.

Figures 56 to 78 illustrate work which has been produced by the mould technique. Attractive and useful household articles can be produced by this method, pots, bowls, trays, platters and dishes, for example, or the basic mould shape can be adapted for more creative work, such as the tortoises illustrated in figures 70 to 72 and the sculpture shown in figure 78.

Figures 73 to 77 show the method of working using a more complex shape as a mould. In this case a glass vase was used. The object is treated with petroleum jelly and covered with papier mâché in the normal way. When dry, a line is drawn across the surface of the papier mâché casing so as to divide it exactly into half, see figure 73. This must be accurately calculated. Next, cut along this line with a sharp knife, as shown in figure 74. Do not attempt to cut through all the layers at once, but rather work carefully along the line to ensure a neat,

straight cut. Try not to damage the surface of the original object underneath. Having cut right round the object, ease each half away from the mould with a palette knife. Trim the top rim edges but do not tidy or trim the joining edges. If required, seal and paint the inside surfaces before carefully fitting the two halves together and joining them along their seams with pasted strips of paper. Use a strong glue (pva) for this, also running some glue into the join as it is worked over. For added strength, apply one further layer of pasted strips over the entire surface. Allow to dry before decorating and finishing, figure 77.

56   Paper pots produced from plastic flower pots

57   Decorative container produced from a flower pot mould

58   Container produced from a plastic mould, painted and decorated with string

59   Papier mâché plate

60   Platter

61   Platter

62   Other platter shapes

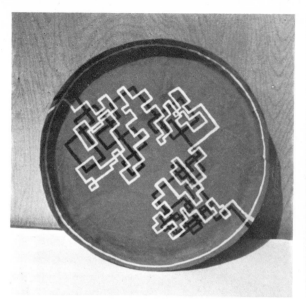

63   Circular tray produced from metal original

64   Tray in use with other containers made from strip and pulp methods

65   Papier mâché fruit bowl

66   Tray: papier mâché, painted with a castle.
The back inscribed 'B. Walton and Co. Warranted
Crusader's Castle 3391'. Mid nineteenth century
Victoria and Albert Museum, Crown Copyright

67 Witch's hat worked over base of thin card

68 Hat: papier mâché over roughly shaped card base, with tissue trim

69 Hats produced from a plastic original

70   Tortoise. Papier mâché bowl adapted by further work in pulp and strip mâché

71   Tortoise: papier mâché bowl developed with pulp and tissue additions

72   Completed version of figure 71

56

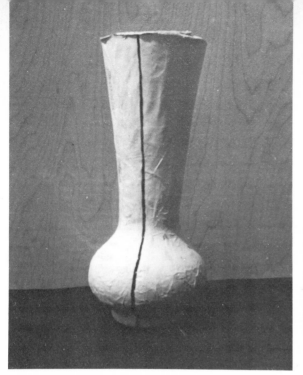

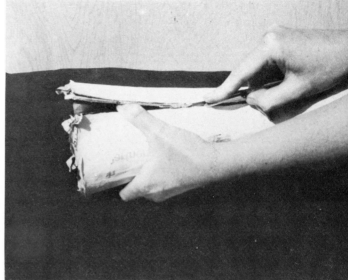

73   Vase: worked in papier mâché over glass original. The line shows a division into halves ready for cutting

74   Cutting through the papier mâché casing with a sharp craft knife

75   Half of the paper mâché form removed from the original mould

76 The two halves ready for trimming and pasting together

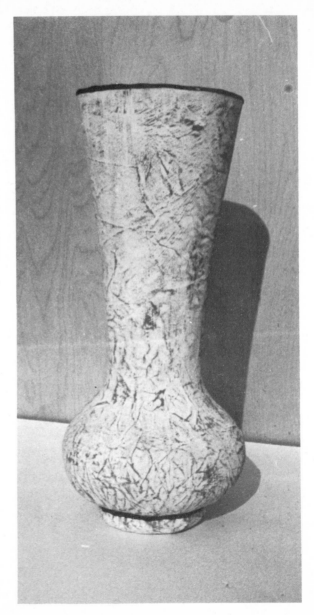

77 The completed vase

5 Using paper pulp

The making of papier mâché pulp or 'mash' is a traditional technique used in the production of decorative modelled forms or utilitarian items duplicated from a mould. Pulp has a different 'feel' and composition from laminated strips and results in an entirely distinct texture. Paper pulp can be applied over basic forms built up with strips or even wire or mesh armatures, it is suitable for filling moulds, and it can be freely modelled, having similar characteristics to clay. The moist pulp surface is ideal for impressed designs, whilst in its dry state the mâché can be incised, carved or smoothed to a very fine finish. Pulp is normally used in a moist state and hence one must allow for a degree of shrinkage due to evaporation.

Making pulp
As before, use torn newspaper, this time making a quantity of pieces each about 25 mm (1 in.) square. The quickest way of making these is to first tear off a pile of 25 mm strips and then to tear through the strips at approximately 25 mm intervals, holding several strips at once and allowing the pieces to fall directly into a bucket or suitably large container. Tearing will expose the fibres of the paper and thus will help in its eventual breaking down into pulp. The amount of torn pieces required often seems deceptively large: an ordinary household bucket (2 gallons; 9 litres) filled with torn paper will make enough pulp for about four puppet heads the size of a fist. Newsprint and similar papers will produce a coarse pulp whilst toilet tissue and paper towelling will give a much softer and finer variety. Pulp can also be made from compressed paper and cardboard cartons and containers, which likewise must be torn into small pieces. Avoid smooth and glossy papers and those which use heavy amounts of ink.

Pour a sufficient amount of hot water into the bucket so as to cover the paper pieces and allow the contents to soak for at least twenty-four hours, stirring occasionally. Alternatively the process can be shortened by using a large, old saucepan and simmering the paper/water mixture over a low heat for several hours, stirring frequently and adding water as necessary to prevent scorching.

Next, drain off the surplus water so that just the soggy paper is left in the bucket. The soaked paper must now be kneaded, pressed and pounded to squeeze out all excess water. The wet mass can be worked with the hands and pressed with a pestle or rolling-pin. Finally squeeze out any remaining water by placing the mash in a sieve, strainer, collander or old stocking.

To turn the wet paper into workable pulp it must now be mixed with a glue or paste solution. Use a paste which has been mixed to a thin, creamy consistency. Flour and water paste, wallpaper paste (wheat paste) or a diluted polymer adhesive are all suitable; add a few drops of oil of wintergreen to flour and water paste to prevent the growth of mould. Add the paste little by little to the wet mash, stirring it in well.

Continue adding paste until a clay-like consistency is obtained. For additional texture, sawdust or sand can be added at this stage. The pulp is now ready for use.

Unless it is stored in a polythene bag or airtight container paper pulp will soon dry out and therefore it is best only to make an amount which is sufficient for immediate requirements and to work the pulp as soon as possible after mixing it. The life of unused pulp can be extended by storing it in a plastic bag in the refrigerator.

Paper pulp is also available as a commercial preparation or *instant mâché* from art and craft suppliers, see p. 17 and the Suppliers list on page 92. Obviously this is much more expensive than the home-made variety but it often dries much harder and may therefore provide a better surface for cutting and carving.

Where pulp is used to model basic forms details can be added with tissue paper which has been saturated in thin glue or liquid starch paste.

Figures 79 to 89 illustrate work produced by using paper pulp. Figure 84 shows two small plastic containers which have been coated with a layer of pulp about 6 mm ($\frac{1}{4}$ in.) thick. When dry, the pulp can be smoothed with abrasive paper to achieve a very fine, even surface, but a useful characteristic of pulp is that in its natural state it gives an interesting textured surface, as in the examples.

Pulp can also be used over a mould and, as in figure 85 can be mixed with saw-dust to create a heavy-textured finish. Like clay,

pulp should not be applied to any great thickness as it will be less likely to dry evenly and thus probably crack. Try not to use thicknesses of more than 1 cm – or about $\frac{1}{2}$ in.

Pulp is ideal for freely modelling small animals and figures, see illustrations 86 and 87. When dry these can be painted and varnished in the usual manner and if necessary attached with a strong adhesive, as with the tail in figure 86.

78 Abstract sculpture made by gluing together segments and shapes cut from papier mâché bowls produced from a mould. Such sculpture can be hand or spray painted and varnished

83   American Treasury figure, paper pulp
Museum of Childhood, Edinburgh

84   Small plastic containers coated with pulp and painted

85   Waste-paper basket: pulp textured with sawdust

86   Pulp model. The tail is a piece of string and the whiskers are nylon bristles from a brush

87   Pulp model

88   Dolls' furniture: painted pulp

89   Beads: hand modelled from pulp, painted and varnished

6   Pasted paper modelling

Using laminated sheets of paper is simple, direct and allows for expressive and imaginative work without a great deal of preparation or the use of elaborate and expensive equipment. Papier mâché has the reputation of being a craft employed only for making useful items and perhaps, as we discovered in our early school years, for puppets and masks. Certainly papier mâché originated as a method for creating functional items, whether a decorative processional mask or a plain canister. However, like basketry, metalwork, woodwork and other similar crafts the competent and imaginative craftsman is able to develop many of the basic skills and apply these to projects which express something more of his personality and which are not determined by a mould or have the design dictated by purely functional issues. In this case, the basic technique of pasting sheets of paper together is used for freely modelling figurative or abstract forms and can be adapted for decorative silhouettes, plaques and relief work.

Method

Select sheets of paper of a size and quality suited to the particular work envisaged. Once more newspaper is a suitable type to use; heavy white cartridge (drawing) paper will give a stronger surface with which to work, whilst water-colour paper has a rougher and more interesting texture and is less likely to buckle or wrinkle. Other papers may also be suitable provided that they are not too thick and therefore allow ease in cutting and shaping. White ticket card can be used but other cardboards are unsatisfactory as they are prone to considerable warping.

Sheets of the selected paper are then pasted one to another to form a thick laminated sheet consisting of six to eight layers. Larger models may require more layers. Use pva adhesive (white glue) or a strong mixture of wallpaper paste (wheat paste). Apply the paste generously with a large brush so that each layer is more than adequately covered, but keep the outer surfaces (top and bottom) dry. The glue is not merely to bind the various layers together but also imparts strength into the fashioned shape; it must therefore be used liberally. Extra strength can be achieved by incorporating a layer of cloth. Allow the pad of laminated paper to dry out somewhat, but whilst it is still damp it can be bent and modelled to shape and will then set in place.

The most successful pasted paper models will combine practical considerations with aesthetic ones. Such models need to be bold in design with emphasis on simple, powerful lines and forms. Shapes may need to be stylised; the technique is ideal for free abstract interpretation.

There are various methods of working, as the laminated sheets of paper can be used on their own, over basic forms or in conjunction with other techniques.

Used by itself the wad of paper can be cut out and fashioned whilst still damp but the model must be so designed that it balances and supports itself. Leave the completed work to dry out thoroughly before painting and varnishing. The surface may be brittle when dry and if so could break. The remedy here is to overwork with squares or strips of papier mâché.

An alternative is to model over a basic form or armature. Cardboard, screwed paper, cardboard tubes and polystyrene shapes can be used as starting points, the layers of paper applied over these. This method will give added stability to the work and is useful when a bulky form is envisaged. Likewise, wire and wire mesh can be used as armatures, methods which are covered in detail in the next section of this book, which deals with papier mâché sculpture. Wire should be bound with masking tape or strips of pasted paper and will need to be fixed to a wooden base with wire staples or nails. The base can also be covered with papier mâché and should be of a size and design consistent with that of the model. However, quite large figures can be made without a base or armature support; particularly if they involve drapery, the figures can be so designed that the papier mâché supports itself.

Simple models made in this way can of course have details added with strip or pulp mâché or tissue paper dipped in glue. The dried surface may be overworked in the usual ways and can be textured by applying a thin layer of plaster, *Polyfilla* (*Spackle*), a plaster and sand mixture, textured pulp or with layers of gesso. Moist plaster surfaces can be worked into with modelling tools, or,

if those are not available, by using the blunt end of a paint brush, a nail, or similar pointed instrument.

Another variant is to cut shapes from the laminated sheets of paper which are bent and modelled individually and subsequently glued together to make one large model. Duplicate shapes can be made by drawing round a template made from thin card. The various layers used in lamination can be cut to a specific shape in this way prior to pasting, and silhouettes thus produced. Silhouettes might be so designed as to be free-standing or could be slotted into a base or attached to a base by means of flaps. Similarly, pasted paper shapes might make use of flaps as a device for securing one to another.

Relief pictures and plaques can also be made by the pasted paper technique. Use a firm support cut from hardboard, masonite or plywood on which to work.

Fabric has been mentioned as a means of strengthening layers of paper; it can, of course, be used on its own to create basic shapes which can later be decorated with paper and fabric trims. Much discarded material is suitable for this and should be coated with undiluted pva adhesive (white glue) prior to cutting and shaping. As before, wet models may need propping up until the glue begins to set. Pva adhesive dries quite quickly and as it does so the form will stiffen and assume the desired shape. Use a thicker, quick-drying paint such as pva on fabric surfaces. It will be unnecessary to seal the surface as the fabric was soaked in

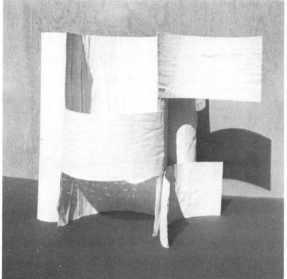

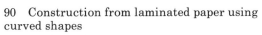

90　Construction from laminated paper using curved shapes

91　Another view of figure 90, after painting

92　Folded construction from laminated newspaper

glue previously.

Laminated sheets of newspaper can also be used to make objects and containers like the one illustrated in figure 93. Paste five or six large sheets of newspaper together and allow to dry. Cut out a suitable length from the laminated sheet and coil this around a tube to form the cylindrical part of the container. Overlap the edges slightly and glue down. Cut a circle from cardboard to fit as the base. Lids can also be made from cardboard and covered by découpage. The container can be painted or covered with a printed paper, such as wallpaper or, as in the example, with corrugated paper.

93 Container made from laminated paper covered with corrugated paper

94 Silhouette: laminated paper

95 Painted silhouette

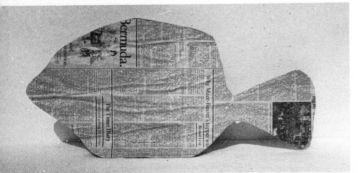

7 Sculpture

Papier mâché has long been associated with the decorative and applied arts but it is only comparatively recently that the technique has been given serious consideration by the practising artist. Modern products and techniques for finishing enable papier mâché to be used for the creation of large, permanent structures which may even be sited out-of-doors. Papier mâché has a number of advantages over wood, metal or stone: in times when the economics of every project has to be seriously considered, it is a relief to find a material which is still inexpensive; papier mâché is also light and therefore very large sculptures are easily manhandled; and an additional advantage is that should the work get damaged it can quickly and easily be repaired. Sculpture will express individual ideas and although, as in all art, certain limits and disciplines must be respected, this work does not have its shape dictated by a mould or the necessity to fulfil functional obligations. Such work is really an extension of that using pasted paper and many of the considerations detailed in the last section will apply equally here.

There is much scope for papier mâché sculpture and the procedures described on the following pages are readily adaptable to particular situations. These techniques can be used to create serious sculpture, to make decorative items, as well as for theatre and play props, for classroom projects, and for display and carnival pieces. All of this work is based on the initial construction of an armature to support the papier mâché

overworking. The armature acts as a skeleton reinforcement and in making it one has to envisage the desired completed form, so that apart from merely functioning as a support, the armature takes into account the distribution of weight and balance. Armatures can be made from various materials, including screwed up paper, paper, stuffed bags, cardboard, cardboard tubes and cartons, balloons, polystyrene (styrofoam) shapes, wire, wire mesh, aluminium foil, and bottles. The armature could be a combination of a number of materials. To make an animal, for example, one might use an armature consisting of a cardboard tube (body), wrapped round with lengths of wire (legs).

Whichever material is employed, the basic procedure is the same: construct the armature; cover with papier mâché strips or pulp; seal; paint and decorate as desired; reseal if necessary. Sculpture which is destined for an outdoor situation must be treated with many layers of lacquer or suitable protective varnish.

Several approaches are detailed below and these may be adapted to suit other materials.

Paper and cardboard
Paper and cardboard can be used in a variety of ways to form effective armatures for simple, small-scale models and shapes. Sheets of newspaper can be twisted or screwed up to form rough shapes which are held in place with string, thread, masking tape or adhesive paper. Cardboard tubes and cartons can be taped or stapled together

before adding papier mâché strips to build up the form. Once the basic shape has been established it is always possible to build up the form either with pulp or by padding with screwed up paper which is bound on with pasted strips. Textural and drapery effects can be achieved by using thick paper or hessian, rag or cheesecloth which has been soaked in pva adhesive (white glue) and allowed to set in a desired modelled form.

Bottles

Bottles are obtainable in different shapes and sizes as well as being of plastic or glass varieties. We are normally very eager to throw away our empty bottles but here is another instance where something which we term as rubbish can be used creatively. Plastic bottles are light, unbreakable and can easily be cut into with a craft knife or sharp scissors. They are therefore the most suitable kind to use for work by children. Glass bottles make more stable armatures but have, of course, a potential danger if knocked over or dropped. When working with glass bottles it is advisable to begin by applying at least two layers of papier mâché so that in the event of it being dropped it will not smash. Pva adhesive will normally stick paper to glass or plastic surfaces but always check that other glues and pastes are suitable. For economy, apply the initial layer with pva adhesive and subsequent layers with paste.

Bottles are ideal for basic figure and animal shapes, whilst sections of plastic bottles and containers can be taped

together and worked over to produce interesting abstract sculptures. See figures 96 to 101.

96 Period figure: papier mâché around a bottle

97 Fish modelled in papier mâché around a
bottle

98 Completed design, as figure 97

99 Alternative design, as figure 97

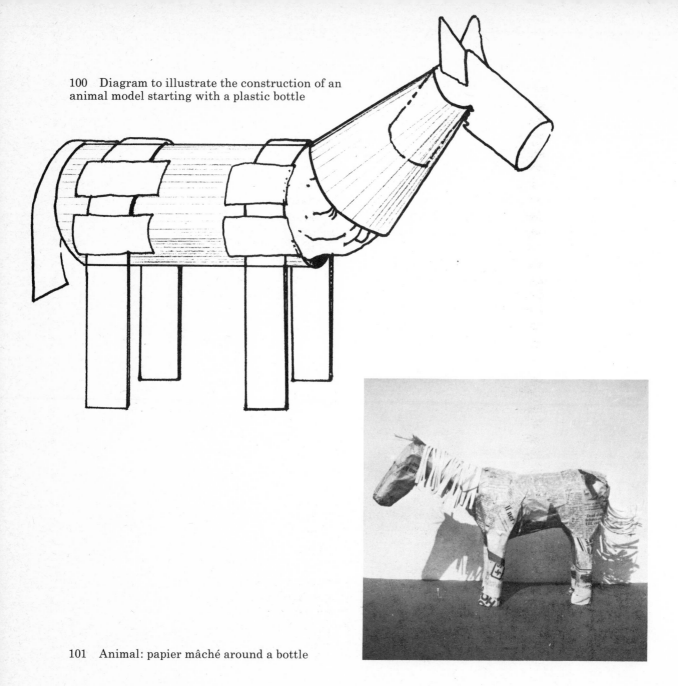

100 Diagram to illustrate the construction of an animal model starting with a plastic bottle

101 Animal: papier mâché around a bottle

Wire

Different types of round and square section
wire are obtainable from suppliers and
hardware stores, although that gleaned from
packing cases and old wire coat-hangers will
be just as effective in constructing an
armature. Aluminium, iron, brass and
copper wire are the most common types;
these are normally sold in coils, either by
weight, for example 3 kg (7 lb), or by
approximate lengths, 23 m (25 yd). The gauge
of wire is similar to that of knitting needles;
20 g is fine, while 12 g cannot be bent
smoothly by hand. Galvanised wire is
recommended for most armature work. A
simple armature could merely consist of a
single length of wire bent to shape and
attached with wire staples to a wooden base
block. Larger, complex shapes might
necessitate the combination of various types
of wire and thus involve some technique for
joining lengths together.

It is essential that the wire armature is
well built and strong enough to support the
weight of papier mâché and perhaps plaster
which is to be applied over it. Joins are
normally the weakest points of a
construction; it is desirable therefore to keep
to the minimum number of joins and to
ensure that those necessary are carefully
made. A reliable method is to 'twist' join
different lengths: overlap the two lengths of
wire at right-angles to each other so that
there is about 25 mm (1 in.) of overlap on
each length, then use a pair of flat nose or
combination pliers to twist the two ends
together. Lengths can also be bound

102   Building a wire armature

together with much thinner wire, such as florist wire or fuse wire. Wire can be taped together with plastic sticky tape, glued with a strong resin glue, such as *Araldite*, or spot soldered. In making the wire framework, respect the nature of the material being used. Lines can be flowing or angular, but do not expect to achieve intricacy. Wire cutters will be essential for trimming the lengths. Thin wire is easily bent by hand or coiled round cylindrical objects. Thicker types may require the use of a vice in which to hold the wire whilst it is bent with pliers or hammered into shape.

The wire 'skeleton' can be employed in a number of ways as the starting point for papier mâché sculpture. Pasted paper strips can easily be bound round the structure until the required thickness is achieved, the work being left to dry before sealing, painting and finishing in the normal way. An alternative is to pad around the framework with screwed up paper before overworking with pasted strips or pulp. The dried paper surface will readily accept thin coats of plaster or *Polyfilla* (*Spackle*) and hence sculptural finishes can be achieved. Models and constructions of this type can be dipped in plaster or the plaster can be applied with a wet knife, spatula or modelling tool. Damp plaster can be textured and worked into whilst dry plaster can be sanded to effect very smooth surfaces.

103   Dragon: strip mâché over wire mesh

104   Detail of figure 103 showing the painted and collaged decoration

Wire mesh

For larger work wire mesh will have the advantage of enabling greater surface area support. Mesh will respond in much the same way as ordinary wire and similar tools will be required. It can be pulled and squeezed, cut and stretched to build a rough foundation shape. Again there are various types and gauges: 13 mm ($\frac{1}{2}$ in.) mesh (chicken wire) is suitable for most work. This is easily fashioned into shape and forms a sturdy supporting structure for the application of pasted paper and plaster. When overworking with pasted strips of paper, build up six or seven layers, applying each layer in a different direction from the last. Use plenty of paste as this will help seal the surface and strengthen it as it dries. Paint and finish in the usual way. A textured finish can be achieved by applying a plaster/sand mixture over the dried papier mâché, or by using lengths of rag or fabric which have been dipped in plaster. See figures 103 to 106.

105   Owl and toadstool: strip mâché over wire mesh

106   Detail of figure 105

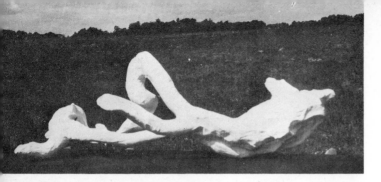

Making large sculptures

Large complex sculptures are possible provided that adequate armature support is used. This may involve building armature structures which combine wood, wire and mesh. Remember that the purpose of the armature is to provide a rigid, balanced framework over which to work, as well as a suitable surface area for applications of papier mâché, bearing in mind that the papier mâché can only achieve a certain thickness. Also, armatures should use lightweight materials so as to keep the total weight of the completed work to a minimum. This may be a most important factor when constructing carnival 'monsters' and similar large decorative pieces which are going to be constantly on the move. Large scale work will follow the normal procedures except, obviously, that larger pieces of pasted paper can be used and that possibly more layers will be required. Indeed, whole sheets of pasted newspaper can be used, but as always, build up the surface by applying these in different directions so as to increase the strength of the finished form.

107
108 } Papier mâché over a 'found' wooden
109 } armature

8   Masks

The use of papier mâché for masks and symbolic forms is long established. Fascinating masks which combine papier mâché with other materials are a feature of Indian and Far Eastern civilisations where the use of elaborate and decorative carved wooden and papier mâché objects is traditional in celebrations and festivals. Other primitive masks, especially those from Africa and South America are carved from wood, although some are modelled in pith which is a pulp substance similar in character and consistency to papier mâché pulp. Masks from all tribes and continents are worth studying and will provide much stimulation and many useful ideas for design.

Originally masks were not merely decorative objects but were made for some special occasion. The ceremonial mask therefore reflected tribal customs and beliefs; there were dance masks, animal masks, harvest masks, spirit masks, funerary masks, hunting masks, death masks, war masks, and so on. All these masks were bold, colourful and decorative with the function of the individual mask emphasised in the exaggerated and often distorted features of the design. Masks, like sculpture, should express a certain idea and, similarly, there is often a need to lay emphasis on certain points whilst perhaps totally ignoring others.

110   Dance mask, Tibet or Bhutan, eighteenth or nineteenth century. Wooden, carved and painted
Victoria and Albert Museum, Crown Copyright

Masks from papier mâché make interesting wall decorations or the mask could be made for some particular event, such as a party, carnival or play. There are various methods of approach and these are outlined below. Most of the methods require a base over which to model the mask and the usual procedure is to apply a layer of wet paper before applying pasted strips, pieces or pulp. Details of the technical processes involved are not given here, since these have been adequately covered in Section 2 of this book.

111   Mask worn to celebrate harvest of wild plums. Saibai, Northern Torres Straits *Royal Scottish Museum, Edinburgh*

112   Mask made over crushed newspaper

Crushed newspaper

A base is made from sheets of newspaper which are tightly crushed into the approximate shape of the mask, be this an oval shape, or something more unusual. Use plenty of paper, making sure that it is firmly crumpled and packed together. Press the newspaper into shape and fix together with sticky tape or string. It is an advantage to tape the base to a table top or similar working surface so that it remains stationary whilst work is in progress. Cover the base with one or two layers of wet paper before proceeding to build up the mask with strips of papier mâché. The wet paper will prevent the papier mâché sticking to the base. Apply six to eight layers of pasted paper, padding out the form where necessary with screwed-up paper soaked in glue. Leave to dry thoroughly before removing the mask from the paper base.

The mask can now be sealed and decorated. If the final layer of pasted paper is one of white newsprint or lining paper then it is possible to work directly on to this without previous coatings of sealer or emulsion.

Making a base from newspaper is a simple and cheap method. The disadvantage of this technique is that the mask is likely to warp whilst drying and therefore this is not a method which is recommended for the accurate reproduction of a base image.

Paper bags

Large, strong brown paper bags are used for base shapes. The paper bag is inflated and its opening gathered and firmly tied with string, held together with an elastic band, or bound round with adhesive tape. If desired, push in the corners of the bag and push and pinch the rest of it into a rough base shape. Work the papier mâché carefully over one side of the bag and leave to dry before untying and trimming off the surplus. With this method there is no need to apply a first layer of wet paper, instead, paste the strips directly on to the bag which will dry to the papier mâché and help strengthen it.

An alternative method is to stuff the bag out with screwed up newspaper which is removed later once the papier mâché has dried. By this means it is possible to work over the entire paper bag surface to create a mask which can be pulled down over the head to completely cover it. Masks made by this method have the advantage of being light and thus suitable for children. Masks so made are likely to warp a little and, as with practically all methods involving papier mâché, there will be a degree of shrinkage as the work dries.

It is worth emphasising here that any mask which is intended to be worn must be so designed as to allow adequate air and ventilation. Ensure that it is not too tight-fitting, especially if it is to be worn for long periods under the hot lights of a theatrical performance. Papier mâché masks and props are a potential fire risk on stage and should be sprayed with an appropriate solution before use. On no account should polythene bags be used; in any case, these are unsuitable for overworking with papier mâché.

Aluminium foil

Use several thicknesses of aluminium foil to model a base which is then covered with papier mâché. Use pva adhesive (white glue) with the first layer of strips so that they stick to the foil. Subsequent layers can use ordinary paste. Leave to dry, trim to shape, patch up and finish in the normal way.

Foil can also be modelled over a real face. Ensure that the model has his eyes closed and work quickly before he runs out of breath!

113   Mask made from aluminium foil impression

114   Mask built up with papier mâché over base of cardboard lids, cartons, etc

Objects

Various objects such as plastic lids, large plates, trays, bowls and platters will serve as moulds over which to work. Protect the object with a coating of petroleum jelly or a layer of wet newspaper before applying the pasted strips. Model on the features by using crumpled up paper soaked in glue, this being fixed in place with pasted strips.

A quicker method is to use laminated sheets of paper which, whilst still wet, are modelled over the object being used as a base. The use of laminated sheets of paper is explained in Section 6 of this book.

Large paper plates can be used as a base and incorporated into the mask to strengthen it. Likewise, papier mâché masks can be modelled over cardboard boxes or cartons, which will act as a frame. Smaller boxes and tubing can be used as the foundation structure for features, see figure 114.

Balloons

The technique of modelling papier mâché over an inflated balloon is a well known one. The balloon is inflated to the desired size before half of its surface is worked over with strips or pulp, or possibly a combination of the two. When the mâché has hardened burst the balloon and remove it. The mask can then be trimmed to shape and decorated.

It is, of course, possible to cover the entire balloon and leave it beneath its coating of papier mâché. Balloons which inflate to a particular shape, such as animal heads, are ideal for this purpose.

Unusual shapes can be made by using several balloons joined together with masking tape.

Wire

Lengths of wire twisted and bent into shape will form a very sturdy framework for covering with papier mâché, and this is an ideal material to use when contemplating larger masks or those such as animal masks which are intended to cover the whole head. Select suitably thick wire and make careful joins. Cover the framework first of all by wrapping pasted strips of paper round it. Ensure that there are no sharp ends which could push through the paper and be dangerous before covering the framework with laminated sheets of paper or wide strips. Use plenty of glue and at least six layers of paper.

Details of different types of wire, their uses and methods of joining them were covered in Section 7, page 73.

Wire mesh

Cut and use the mesh in the same way as that described for papier mâché sculpture, page 75. Wire mesh provides the best surface for large masks but it does, of course, add to their weight. If possible, when the mask is dry, turn it over and cover the inside with a further one or two layers of pasted paper. This will make a smoother, neater finish and give additional strength.

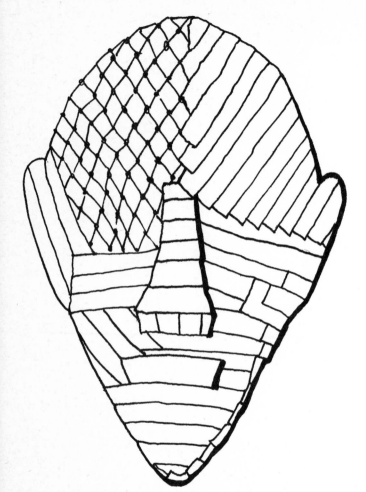

Clay

For realism and detail, modelling clay is an excellent medium to use. Begin by modelling the base in clay. The features need to be exaggerated as subsequent layers of newspaper will tend to level them out. Coat the clay with petroleum jelly before applying the papier mâché strips. Ensure that the first layer of strips is pushed well into the variations of the surface. Build up the mask with about six layers of paper. When dry, it should be possible to remove the mask carefully from its clay mould, so that this can be used again for another mask. Patch up any weak places before sealing and decorating.

Plasticine

This is used in exactly the same way as clay. Once again the features must be exaggerated. Plasticine can be used over and over again and, as it remains pliable, alterations are easily made to the basic form.

Plaster

If a quantity of identical masks is required then it may be advantageous to make a plaster mould. The method is the same as that described on page 49.

115   Diagram to show the application of papier mâché strips over a wire mesh base

9 Puppets

Like masks, the use of papier mâché is traditional for making puppets. Most of the methods described for making masks can be adapted for modelling puppets and will be equally fascinating to young and old alike.

Using a paper tube
A roll of thick paper is used to act as a neck and also the central support for the head. The roll should be large enough for one or two fingers to be inserted into it. Secure the roll with brown gummed paper or strips of pasted paper. Alternatively start with a length of cardboard tubing. Build up a rough shape over the top half of the tube. This can be modelled with pulp, built up with newspaper soaked in glue, or simply formed by winding strips of pasted paper round the tube in different directions. The purpose of this rough shape is to form a firm support for the detailed modelling of the puppet. The work should be left to dry; when it is really hard work over with pulp or screwed up pieces of paper soaked in glue. The final details should be bold and somewhat exaggerated to allow for the usual shrinkage. The creation of bold characteristics and features is especially important if the puppet is being designed for use in a puppet theatre.

Allow the puppet to dry out thoroughly before smoothing the surface with a fine abrasive paper and painting. Again, it is necessary to paint in an exaggerated, bold style to emphasise expression and character so that these qualities appear obvious from a distance. Hair and other details can be glued

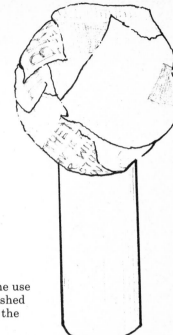

116 Diagram to show the use of crushed newspaper pushed into a cardboard tube as the basis for a puppet head

on to the main form. Real hair can be used, or alternatively, frayed string, jute, raffia or wool. Animal puppets might make use of animal fur and feathers. The main body of the puppet is normally made from fabric or felt and designed so that it is large enough to cover the hand. Details can be sewn on to the fabric body and this lightly attached to the head. It is possible to so design the puppet that the head merely drops or slots into an opening in the body and therefore allows the interchange of head with different bodies.

Plasticine
A puppet modelled from a plasticine mould is hollow and thus has the advantage of being much lighter and less top-heavy than

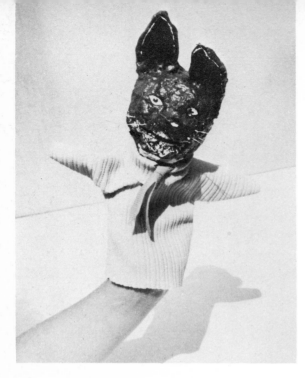

117 Fox puppet made by a girl aged 7

118 Puppet head. Note the necessity to exaggerate features, both in their formation and painting

the solid type formed round a tube. The head and neck are first modelled from plasticine; as usual the features are emphasised as subsequent layers of paper will tend to even out their effect. Cover the modelled form first with a layer of thin wet tissue paper and then with at least six layers of pasted paper. Use small pieces of pasted paper, ensuring that these are carefully pushed into the variations of the surface. Allow the paper to dry and then cut the model in half, using a sharp craft knife. Do this slowly and carefully, working round the model so as to make a clean cut through the paper casing. Children should not be allowed to use sharp knives. Having cut all the way round, it should be possible to separate the two halves and then take out the plasticine, which can be re-used. Small amounts of plasticine may be left to strengthen any prominent features, such as the nose. The two parts are joined together with small strips of pasted paper and, when dry, the puppet can be sandpapered and painted in the usual way.

A similar technique is to use an object such as a plastic toy as the basic mould. Only the head need be worked over. When the papier mâché shape is removed its edges can be trimmed and the form adapted by further papier mâché work or by adding fabric so that the desired puppet shape is achieved. The object must first be coated with a thin layer of *Vaseline*; follow the procedure outlined in Section 4.

10 Other ideas

The previous sections have dealt with
specific ideas and techniques related to the
use of papier mâché. It will be apparent that
papier mâché is a versatile medium
adaptable to a particular functional,
educational or artistic context. The
remaining examples illustrated in this book
are those which do not readily fall into
preceding categories and headings and thus
form a collection of their own; each
example will suggest a variety of
interpretations and may inspire the reader
along further lines of exploration.

Paper flowers
These can be made from laminated sheets of
pasted paper. Paste five or six sheets of
newspaper together in the way described in
Section 6. When dry, this will form a sturdy
laminated sheet of paper similar in thickness
and handling characteristics to thin card,
only very much cheaper to produce. Flower
shapes can be cut from the laminated paper
and these painted, decorated and varnished.
Tissue paper dipped in adhesive and other
pasted papers can be used to model details.
Stems are made by binding pasted paper
around lengths of strong wire.

Large flowers can be built up by a
sectional method; each petal, for example,
could be made as an individual unit.

Jewellery
Bracelets can be built by strip or pulp
method around a bottle, cardboard tubing, or
similar cylindrical object. Select the object
to suit the size (diameter) of bracelet

119   Paper flowers, laminated paper

120   Bracelet: papier mâché decorated with braid
and beads

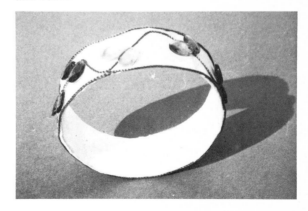

desired. Remember to treat the surface of the object with petroleum jelly, or to start with wet, unpasted paper in order to prevent the mâché sticking to it. Remove, trim and patch up in the usual way. Beads, small shells and other decorative items can be set into the wet mâché or glued on afterwards, as can braid, coloured string and fabric. See figure 120.

Other jewellery, such as beads, pendants and broaches, is easily made from pulp mâché. The basic shapes are made from pulp and allowed to dry before being smoothed with fine abrasive paper, painted, decorated and possibly varnished. Holes for beads which are to be strung together are made with a thin knitting needle or similar item. Broaches can incorporate a clip or safety pin which is set into the wet mâché. Remember always to use a stronger adhesive, perhaps an epoxy resin or contact adhesive, for attaching decorative items to a basic papier mâché surface.

See also figures 41 and 89.

Mobiles

Shapes cut from laminated paper can be painted, decorated and suspended on lengths of thread, string or thin wire to form a mobile.

Mobiles consist of loosely attached, balanced shapes which are agitated by air currents. They can be made from all types of paper, card and foil as well as these combined with other materials, such as tin, wood and polystyrene. Papier mâché strips or pulp can be worked over a thin shape cut from plywood, hardboard (*masonite*) or cardboard in order to create a modelled, textured surface. The composition of a mobile is concerned with the qualities of rhythm and balance and its design may well be influenced to a great extent by these two considerations. Avoid large, heavy shapes which obviously will require more than a mere draught to agitate them. A well-constructed mobile will be constantly changing, full of expression.

The various parts of a mobile can be suspended from a main horizontal wire which, in turn, is suspended from a hook or screw in the ceiling, or similar suitable projection.

Costumes

Although restricting in movement papier mâché costumes are fun both to make and to wear for carnival occasions. Care must of course be taken to ensure that the wearer's sight and breathing are not restricted. Remember that such costumes could be a potential fire hazard.

Relief work

Papier mâché is an ideal material for modelling relief maps, making decorative plaques, or for texturing areas of a painting.

Build the relief design on a firm base such as hardboard (*masonite*). Use pva adhesive for the foundation layers in order to ensure that the paper sticks securely to the base. Really thick areas should be built up gradually; if using pulp, apply about 25 mm (1 in.) at a time, allowing this to dry out

121 Papier mâché 'vegetable' costumes made for
a carnival. Designed by Elizabeth Leyh, Stacey
Hill Farm Studio, Milton Keynes

122 Detail of 'mushroom' hat

somewhat before adding more pulp. An alternative method is to use screwed up paper as padding, taping this securely to the base with pasted lengths of paper. For a really firm finish, coat the entire surface with pva adhesive, gesso, or a thin layer of plaster. In similar fashion, pulp and crinkled pasted paper can be applied to a painting support to create textures. When dry, the paper can be overpainted in the normal way.

Découpage and collage

Découpage and collage are techniques allied to papier mâché in that they use pasted paper. In this context découpage is the use of specifically selected and cut papers with which to cover an object or surface, see figures 124 and 125. A basic papier mâché surface could therefore be decorated in a découpage way using printed papers, such as wallpaper, or particular shapes cut from magazines, as illustrated.

Paper collage can be defined as picture-making by gluing selected torn or cut areas of paper to a backing support. This can involve newspaper as well as all kinds of textured and coloured papers. Association of shapes, colours, words or pictures is fundamentally important to the composition.

123 Farm: model with pulp, cardboard, straw, etc

The result can be of an intellectual, pictorial or purely aesthetic nature.

Readers who wish to develop these and other ideas associated with papier mâché will find books on these subjects recommended in the list of further reading which follows this section.

124 Papier mâché plate decorated with découpage and varnished

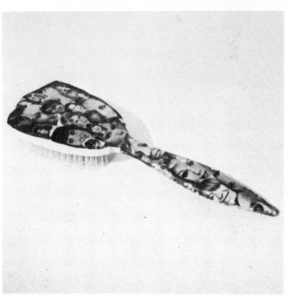

125 Hair brush: découpage

Further reading:

Papier mâché and allied techniques

Art and Design in Papier Mâché, Karen Kuykendall, Hearthside Press, New York; Kaye and Ward, London

Papier Mâché Artistry, Dona Z Meilach, George Allen & Unwin, London; Crown, New York

Starting with Papier Mâché, Chester Jay Alkema, Sterling Publishing Co, Inc, New York; Oak Tree Press, London

Creative Papier Mâché, Betty Lorrimer, Studio Vista, London

The Art of Papier Mâché, Carla and John B Kenny, Chilton, London and New York

Papier Mâché and How to Use It, Mildred Anderson, Sterling Publishing Co Inc, New York; Oak Tree Press, London

Exploring Papier Mâché, Victoria Bedford Betts, Davis Publications Inc, Worcester, Massachusetts USA; Oak Tree Press, London

Contemporary Découpage, Thelma R Newman, George Allen & Unwin, London; Crown, New York

Découpage, Dorothy Harrower, Barrows, New York

Masks, Chester Jay Alkema, Sterling Publishing Co Inc, New York; Oak Tree Press, London

Make a Mask, Joan Peters and Anna Sutcliffe, Batsford, London

Collage: Personalities, Concepts, Techniques, Harriet Jarvis and Rudi Blesh, Pitman, London and New York

Approaches to College, Warren Farnworth, Batsford, London

The Technique of Collage, Helen Hutton, Batsford, London; Watson-Guptill, New York (out of print)

Paper Collage, Robin Capon, Batsford, London

Creative Paper Craft, Ernst Röttger, Batsford, London; Van Nostrant Reinhold, New York

Creating with Paper, Pauline Johnson, Kaye and Ward, London

Sculpture in Paper, Ralph Fabri, Watson-Guptill, New York

Take an Egg Box, Richard Slade, Faber, London

Art From Scrap Materials, Robin Capon, Batsford, London

Carton Craft, Richard Slade, Faber, London

Creating with Plaster, Dona Z Meilach, Blandford Press, London

Suppliers

Great Britain

Paints, crayons, inks, papers and general art materials
Fred Aldous, 37 Lever Street, Manchester M60 1UX
E J Arnold (School Supplier), Butterley Street, Leeds LS10 1AX
Dryad Limited, Northgates, Leicester LE1 4QR
Educational Supply Association, Pinnacles, Harlow, Essex
Margros Limited, Monument House, Woking, Surrey
Reeves and Sons Limited, Lincoln Road, Enfield, Middlesex
George Rowney and Company Limited, 10 Percy Street, London W1
Winsor and Newton Limited, Wealdstone, Harrow, Middlesex

Papier mâché pulp
E J Arnold, Butterley Street, Leeds LS10 1AX
James Galt and Co Ltd, Brookfield Road, Cheadle, Cheshire SK8 2PN

Gesso powder and Barbola Paste
Winsor and Newton Limited, Wealdstone, Harrow, Middlesex

Powdered pigments, linseed oil, whiting
A Leete and Co Ltd, 129 London Road, London SE1

Linseed oil
Boots Chemist Ltd *and artists suppliers as above*

Adhesives
Gloy Schools Service Association Adhesives Limited, 8th Avenue Works, Manor Park, London E12 (for *Gloy* multiglue)
Copydex Limited, 1 Torquay Street, Harrow Road, London W2 (for *Copydex*)
Liberta Imex Limited, Liberta House, Scotland Hill, Sandhurst, Camberley, Surrey (for UHU)
Margros Limited, Monument House, Monument Way West, Woking, Surrey (for *Marvin Medium*)

Polymer adhesives are also available from general suppliers listed above. Other glues are available from stationers and hardware stores

Paper varnish
From stationers and general art suppliers

Other varnishes, household paints, lacquer, aerosol paints, abrasive paper, large brushes, wire mesh, etc from hardware stores, Do-it-Yourself Shops, motor accessory stores and F W Woolworth

Plastic buckets and bowls
From hardware and department stores

USA

General art materials
Grumbacher, 460 West 34th Street, New York
The Morilla Company Inc, 43 21st Street, Long Island City, New York and 2866 West 7th Street, Los Angeles, California

New Masters Art Division, California
Products Corporation, 169 Waverley Street,
Cambridge, Massachusetts
Stafford-Reeves Inc, 626 Greenwich Street,
New York NY 100 14
Winsor and Newton Inc, 555 Winsor Drive,
Secaucus, New Jersey 07094
Mail Order service is available from:
Arthur Brown Inc, 2 West 46th Street, New
York, NY 10036
A I Friedman, 25 West 45th Street, New
York, NY 10036

Papier Mâché mixes and adhesives
Riverside Paper Corp, Appleton, Wisconsin
54911 (Décomâché)
Henkel, Inc, Teaneck, New Jersey 07666
(Metylan paste)

Adhesives
Harrower House of Découpage, River Road,
Upper Black Eddy, Bucks County,
Pennsylvania, 18972 (Mucilage for
découpage)
3M Company, St Paul, Minnesota 55119
(3M Spra-ment rubber cement)
Miracle Adhesive Corp, Bellmore, NY 11710
(Water clear epoxy)
Slomons Lab Inc, 32–45 Hunters Point
Avenue, Long Island City, NY 11101 (*Sobo*
and *Quik*)
Eagle Pencil Company, Danbury,
Connecticut (for *Marvin Medium*)
Stafford-Reeves Inc and Winsor and Newton
Inc will supply pva adhesive

Paints
Barrett Varnish Company, 1532 South 50th
Street, Cicero, Illinois 60650 (exotic spray
paints)
The American Crayon Company (Dixon),
Sandusky, Ohio 44870 (*Prang* acrylic paint)
Permanent Pigments, 27000 Highland
Avenue, Cincinnati, Ohio 45212 (*Liquitex*
acrylic paints, emulsions and modelling
paste)

Varnishes
Cunningham Arts Products Inc, 1564
McCurdy Drive, Stone Mountain, Georgia
30083 (*Flourish*)
McCloskey's Varnishes, Philadelphia,
Pennsylvania 19136
Miracle Adhesive Corp, Bellmore, NY 11710
(Miracle Epoxy)
New York Bronze Powder Company, 519
Dowd Avenue, Elizabeth, New Jersey 07201
(Polyurethane spray)

Papers and decorative trims
Available from most general suppliers, and
William E Wright Company, West Warren,
Massachusetts 01092 (self-adhesive papers
and trims)
Andrew-Nelson-Whitehead, 7 Laight Street,
New York, NY 10013 (exotic papers)

All other materials from local arts and
crafts stores, hardware and drug stores.

Index

J

Japanned papier mâché;
   figure 2
Jennens and Bettridge; figures
   4, 16, 82
Jewellery 85; figures 41, 89, 120
Joining 50

K

Kneading paper 59

L

Lace 27
Laminated sheets 65, 66, 68, 81,
   85, 86; figures 90–92, 94, 95
Laminated strips 45, 86
Laquer 25, 29, 69
Latex paint 23, 27
Lining paper 79
Linseed oil 22
Liquid porcelain 29
Lumps 31

M

Magazines 15, 88; figures 35,
   124, 125
Maps 86
Masks 33, 77; figures 110–115
Masking tape 66, 69, 81
Masonite (see hardboard)
Mash (see pulp)
Match boxes; figures 31, 32
Metal surfaces 30
Metallic spray paint 27
Mobiles 86
Mould growth 19, 59
Moulds 43, 50, 59
Mouse; figure 86
Mother-of-pearl; figure 80
Music Canterbury; figure 80

N

Newspaper 13, 15, 59, 65, 68, 69

O

Offsetting 25
Oil paint 27
Oil of wintergreen 59
Opaque finishes 27
Origin of papier mâché 9
Overworking 30, 43, 75; figures
   18–22
Owl; figure 106

P

Padding with paper 31
Paint compatibility 24
Painting 24
Palette knife 45
Papers 15
Paper bags 79
Paper doilies 27
Paper flowers 85; figure 119
Paper plates 81
Paper racks; figures 79, 82
Paper towelling 16
Paper varnish 28
Pasted paper 65, 69, 75, 76;
   figures 90–95
Pendants 86
Pestle 59
Petroleum jelly 43, 50, 81, 86;
   figure 47
Plaques 49, 65, 66
Plaster 43, 49, 66, 73, 74, 82, 88
Plaster mixture 23, 75
Plaster mould 49; 82
Plastic bottles 30, 70; figures
   100, 101
Plastic bowls 43
Plastic buckets 13, 19
Plastic tape 74
Plastic toys 84
Plasticine 49, 82, 83, 84
Plate; figure 59
Platter; figures 60, 61, 62
Play props 69, 79
Plywood 86

Pole screens; figure 4

Polyfilla 23, 66, 74
Polystyrene 13, 30
Polyurethane varnish 28
Potato-printed papers 27
Powder paint 25
Primers 23
Primitive masks 77; figures 110,
   111
Printed papers 16, 33, 88
Pulp 59, 66, 78, 81, 85, 86;
   figures 79–89
Puppets 13, 83
PVA medium 19, 23, 28, 31, 33,
   44, 59, 65, 66, 70, 86

R

Rag 70, 75
Relief work 65, 66, 86
Rolling-pin 59

S

Sand 60, 75
Sawdust 60; figure 85
Sculpture 33, 69; figures 78,
   107–109
Sealing 23
Separating medium 43
Shellac varnish 29
Shells 14, 27, 86
Silhouettes 65, 66; figures 94, 95
Simmering 59
Size 23
Slotting 66
Soaking paper 59
Spot-soldering 74
Spray diffuser 25
Spray gun 25
Spraying 24, 25
Stamps 33; figure 32
Stapling 69
Snuff-box; figure 79
Starch 60
Sticky tape 74